INTERNATIONAL SOCIETY OF CRYPTOZOOLOGY

FIELD GUIDE

to the

SASQUATCH

David George Gordon

SASQUATCH BOOKS

Seattle, Washington

Printed in the United States of America

Cover design and illustration: Dugald Stermer
Text illustrations and maps: © 1992 by Joyce Bergen
Composition: Scribe Typography

Library of Congress Cataloging in Publication Data

Gordon, David G. (David George), 1950–
    Field guide to the sasquatch : follow in the footsteps of North America's most elusive animal / by David George Gordon.
        p.   cm.
    At head of title: International Society of Cryptozoology.
    Includes bibliographical references.
    ISBN 0-912365-54-4 : $4.95
    1. Sasquatch.   I. International Society of Cryptozoology.
II. Title.
QL89.2.S2G67   1992
001.9'44--dc20   92-11435
                                                                          CIP

Published by Sasquatch Books
1931 Second Avenue
Seattle, Washington 98101
(206) 441-5555

Other titles in the Sasquatch Field Guide series:

The Audubon Society
Field Guide to the Bald Eagle

The Oceanic Society
Field Guide to the Gray Whale

American Cetacean Society
Field Guide to the Orca

Great Bear Foundation
Field Guide to the Grizzly Bear

Contents

Introduction

In the introduction to my last book, *The Audubon Society Field Guide to the Bald Eagle* (Sasquatch Books, 1991), I wrote about the difficulty of producing a guide to an endangered animal species. In this book I find myself facing an even greater task: that of describing a creature I've never seen and whose very existence I can neither confirm nor deny.

To my knowledge, this book is the first go-and-see guide to a "cryptid," an animal subject of "cryptozoological" scrutiny. "Cryptozoology," a word coined in the late 1950s by Bernard Heuvelmans, the co-founder of the International Society of Cryptozoology (ISC), is defined as the science of hidden animals. According to the ISC's published bylaws, a cryptozoologist's quarry includes "animals of unexplained form or size, or unexpected occurrence in time or space."

Familiar cryptids include Nessie, the oft-sighted monster of Scotland's Loch Ness; the Abominable Snowman, or Yeti, of Tibet; and, closer to home, Ogopogo, a purported denizen of British Columbia's Lake Okanagan. Until physical proof of these creatures' existence is obtained, none are likely to be formally recognized by science. While it is considered worthy of close examination by the ISC, the Sasquatch has yet to be acknowledged as real by the scientific community at large.

What exactly is a Sasquatch? Physical descriptions of this puzzling cryptid can differ substantially from one alleged eyewitness to the next. Still, there are enough similarities among the more than 800 Sasquatch sightings in the Northwest to put together a generalized profile of the beast. Overall, the best such profile is contained in Appendix D of the *Washington Environmental Atlas*, a reference work produced by the U.S. Army Corps of Engineers. According to this authoritative source, the Sasquatch is "an ape-like creature, standing between 8 and 12 feet tall, weighing in excess of 1,000 pounds and taking strides of up to 6 feet.... Reported to feed on vegetation and some meat, the Sasquatch is covered with long hair, except for the face and hands, and has a distinctly humanlike form. Sasquatch is very agile and powerful, with the endurance to cover a vast range in search of food, shelter and others of its kind. It is apparently able to see at night and is extremely shy, leaving minimal evidence of its presence."

But can we safely say that such a stupendous creature exists anywhere outside of our minds? The Army Corps of Engineers takes a cautious stance: "If the Sasquatch is purely legendary, the legend is likely to be a long time dying. On the other hand, if the Sasquatch does exist, then with the Sasquatch hunts being mounted and the increasing human population, it seems likely that some hard evidence may soon be at hand."

Should this hard evidence ever appear, the Sasquatch is likely to join the list of once unfamiliar creatures that, following their initial discovery and capture, became common fixtures in zoos, museums, and elementary school texts. Consider the gorilla, discounted as a native myth by scientists—despite numerous African tribal reports and the testimony of several European eyewitnesses—until the mid-1800s. Or take the unexpected discovery of the coelacanth, a "living fossil" fish first found off the South African coast in 1938; or Megamouth, a totally new species, genus, and family of shark accidentally snagged in the sea anchor of a U.S. Navy vessel off the Hawaiian Islands in 1976.

Coming up with hard evidence of the Sasquatch's existence may prove more difficult than any member of the Army Corps of Engineers could imagine. We know little more about Sasquatch today than we did when the *Washington Environmental Atlas* was first compiled, almost 20 years ago. The *Field Guide to the Sasquatch* was written to brief readers on the current state of Sasquatch studies. For help with this task, I am most grateful to John Green and other Sasquatch scholars who so freely shared their knowledge of this poorly understood animal. For help in addressing the book's second purpose—offering practical information and advice for would-be Sasquatch seekers—I am thankful to J. Richard Greenwell and other ISC members who reviewed the manuscript. From my conversations with Richard, I learned that absence of evidence is not necessarily evidence of an absence.

David George Gordon

A Cryptid of Many Names

The names Bigfoot and Sasquatch are used interchangeably by the press in the Northwest. Strictly speaking, however, "Bigfoot" refers to unidentified humanlike creatures of Washington, Oregon, and northern California. A relatively recent appellation, this apt name first appeared in the caption to a photo of a cast made from a supposed Sasquatch footprint, taken by the *Humboldt Times* of Eureka, California, in August 1958. When the picture and an accompanying story were picked up by the Associated Press, the name Bigfoot became widespread.

The word Sasquatch has been in use for centuries, first by the natives of the lower Fraser River Valley in British Columbia and more recently by hikers and hominid hunters north of the 49th parallel. (Hominids are the family of bipedal primate mammals that includes recent man, man's immediate ancestors, and related forms.) The name Sasquatch was popularized by J. W. Burns, a teacher on the Chehalis Indian Reserve east of Vancouver, British Columbia, whose stories about the region's hairy monsters appeared in numerous newspapers and magazines of the 1920s.

One of the oldest written descriptions of a Sasquatch-like creature comes from José Mariaño Mozino, a naturalist who accompanied Juan Francisco de la Bodega y Quadra during his exploration of the British Columbian coast in 1792. Mozino wrote of the Matlox, an "inhabitant of the mountainous country, of whom all have an unspeakable terror. They figure it has a monstrous body, all covered with black animal hair; the head like a human; but the eye teeth very sharp and strong, like those of the bear; the arms very large, and the toes and fingers armed with large curved nails. His howls fell to the ground those who hear them, and he smashes into a thousand pieces the unfortunate on whom a blow of his hand falls."

Mozino's description could also apply to the Boqs, a familiar figure to the Bella Coola Indians of British Columbia's central coast. According to anthropologist T. F. McIlwraith of the University of Toronto, the Boqs "somewhat resembles a man, its hands especially, and the region around the eyes being distinctly human. It walks on its hind legs, in a stooping posture, its long arms swinging below its knees: in height it is rather less than the average man. With the exception of its face, the entire body is covered with long hair, the growth being especially profuse on the chest, which is large, corresponding to the great strength of the animal."

Large, hairy beings appear in the legends of many other Northwest Indian tribes. The Huppa of northern California's Klamath Mountains spoke of the Oh-mah-'ah (often shortened to Omah), while Washington's Upper Skagit people believed in Kala'litabiqw, a spirit who had moss growing on his head and could cross the Cascade mountains in a single stride. Other Northwest tribes kept their youngsters close to home with tales of the Steta'l, a dreaded race of mountain giants that kidnapped children and could drive adults insane.

"The Tsiatko are described as a gigantic size, their feet 18 inches long and shaped like a bear's," observed George Gibbs, describing the nemesis of western Washington's Nisqually tribe in 1856. "They wear no clothes, but the body is covered with hair like that of a dog, only not so thick.... They are said to live in the mountains, in holes underground, and to smell bad. They come down chiefly in the fishing season, at which time the Indians are excessively afraid of them.... Their voices are like that of an owl, and they possess the power of charming, so that those hearing them become demented or fall down in a swoon."

But are the descriptions of these strange beings based on actual sightings of Sasquatches or their kin? For Sasquatch seekers, this nagging question must be addressed. "It is certainly true that we anthropologists have generally dumped Sasquatch-like beings into a category 'supernaturals' and let it go at that," writes Wayne Suttles of Portland State University in an article in *Northwest Anthropological Research Notes*. "Since we Europeans, scientifically trained or not, operate with a dichotomy real/ mythical or natural/supernatural, we are inclined to place these creatures that are not part of our 'real' world into our category 'mythical' or 'supernatural.'"

Like so many cryptozoological questions, this one will only be answered when scientifically acceptable proof of the Sasquatch's existence is put forth.

Close Friends or Distant Cousins?

Reports of possible apelike relatives of the Sasquatch come from all centuries and all corners of the world. The 10th-century Arab Maqdisi wrote of the Nsanas, a name still used to describe wild men of the Pamirs, Turkestan, and the desert regions between Kashmir, Tibet, and China. In Mongolia's Gobi Desert, nomadic tribesmen continue to speak of the Almas, odd upright-walking beings with sloping foreheads, large jaws, prominent eyebrows, and other characteristics of Neanderthals. Add to this list the russet-haired Agogwe of Tanzania, the 5½-foot-tall (1.7 m) Kakundakari of the Congo, the diminutive Orang-Pendek of Indonesia, and the Kung-Lu and Tok of Burma, and you've barely begun to assemble the roster of near-humans purported to coexist with the world's numerous and diverse human cultures.

Perhaps the most widely publicized of all unexplained "man-apes" is the Yeti, or Abominable Snowman, of the Himalaya of India, Nepal, and Tibet. Alleged to live in caves at altitudes between 14,000 and 20,000 feet (4,200 – 6,100 m) or, at lower altitudes, in impenetrable thickets of montane forests, this creature is said to be 4 to 6 feet tall (1.2 – 1.8 m), with a stooped posture, reddish hair, and facial features similar to an ape's or a monkey's. Like those of the Sasquatch, published descriptions of the Yeti are highly variable and largely secondhand. The relationship between the two possible hominids has yet to be determined.

Rumors of strange, apelike animals in the New World started circulating with the arrival of European settlers. Sharing his views on the 5-foot-tall (1.5 m) Didi of the Guianas, the 16th-century chronicler Sir Walter Raleigh wrote, "For my owne part I saw them not, but I am resolved that so many people did not all combine or forethinke to make the report." Since Raleigh's time, stories of close to a dozen New World hominids have come to light, among them Guatemala's Sisimite and the Dwendi of Belize, not to mention the giant Mapinguary of Brazil, which leaves 20-inch (.5 m) tracks and kills cattle by tearing out their tongues.

A Sasquatch Family Tree

Similarities in physical form and behavior suggest that the Sasquatch is a member of the primate order, a taxonomic grouping of warm-blooded animals with grasping hands and feet, forward-facing eyes, and well-developed brains. However, without an actual specimen to examine, it is impossible to authoritatively assign the Sasquatch a rung on the evolutionary ladder or branch of the primate family tree.

The 14 families of primates are divided into two suborders. Informally known as the "almost monkeys," the **prosimians** — lemurs, lorises, and tarsiers — are small, nocturnal tree-dwellers. As their name implies, the **anthropoids** — monkeys and apes — share certain physical and behavioral traits with humans. They are diurnal and tend to spend more time on the ground than

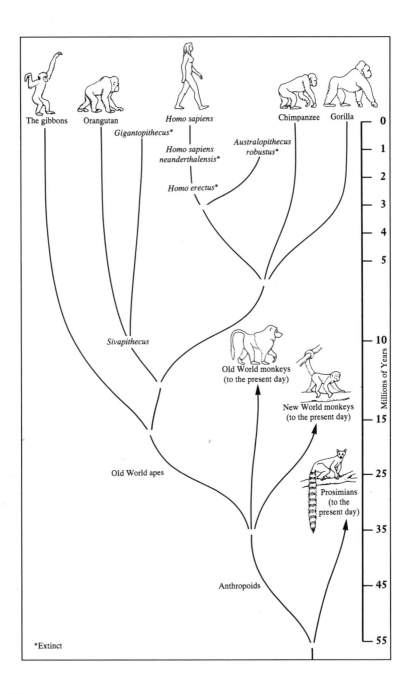

The gibbons Orangutan *Homo sapiens* Chimpanzee Gorilla

*Gigantopithecus**

*Homo sapiens
neanderthalensis** *Australopithecus
robustus**

*Homo erectus**

Sivapithecus

Old World monkeys
(to the present day)

New World monkeys
(to the present day)

Old World apes

Prosimians
(to the
present day)

Anthropoids

Millions of Years

0
1
2
3
4
5

10

15

25

35

45

55

*Extinct

their prosimian relatives. Most anthropoids, especially those from the Old World (Africa and Asia), are considerably larger than the prosimians.

The anthropoid suborder contains three superfamilies: New World (South and Central American) monkeys, Old World monkeys, and Old World apes. Included in this third group are the tailless primates: the gibbons (genus *Hylobates*) and orangutan (genus *Pongo*) of Southeast Asia and the gorilla (genus *Gorilla*) and chimpanzee (genus *Pan*) of Africa. Also included is the hominid family, of which our own genus, *Homo*, is a part, as well as any other tailless, upright-walking species, either living or dead, that may have evolved after our human and ape ancestors separated. Because this separation took place roughly 5 million to 10 million years ago, there is a paucity of early hominid remains; to date, no one has been able to definitively trace the bloodlines of ancient hominids or fully determine the relationship between humans and modern-day apes.

The Sasquatch may have evolved from one of these long-gone hominid stocks, possibly *Homo erectus* (Java or Peking man), *Homo sapiens neanderthalensis* (commonly known as Neanderthal man), or *Australopithecus robustus* (an early human predecessor from South Africa). Fossil remains of Neanderthal man tell us that this genus may have hung on the longest of the three, dying out some 30,000 to 40,000 years ago—the recent past in paleontological terms. But many cryptozoologists conjecture that relict populations of one or more of these genera may have somehow survived, a view that would account for most contemporary sightings of hairy hominids around the world.

In excavations in China and Vietnam, scientists have uncovered a fourth possible forebear of the Sasquatch. This latest candidate is the genus *Gigantopithecus*, which possibly shares a common 8 million-year-old ancestor, *Sivapithecus*, with the orangutan. Known only from the fossil remains of four massive jawbones and a thousand extremely large teeth, *Gigantopithecus* is believed to have been the largest primate that ever lived, standing 10 feet (3 m) tall on the Pliocene landscape, some 6 million to 7 million years ago. It has been estimated that *Gigantopithecus* may have walked the earth as recently as the late mid-Pleistocene epoch, roughly 500,000 years ago, perhaps as recently as 300,000 years ago.

But did *Gigantopithecus* really disappear from our planet? The mighty ancestor of the Sasquatch may in fact have enlarged its range during the Pleistocene ice age, when a land bridge from Alaska to Siberia connected the New World with the Old. Perhaps this giant hominid merely went "undercover," reemerging periodically from the forests and fields of North America. This is the contention of at least one Sasquatch scholar, anthropologist Grover Krantz, who has proposed that the scientific name for one of the fossil species, *Gigantopithecus blackii*, be applied to the Sasquatch of the Pacific Northwest.

Krantz's proposal has met strong opposition from several other scientists, including Russell Ciochon, one of the foremost authorities on *Gigantopithecus* fossils. In his book *Other Origins: The Search for the Giant Ape in Human Prehistory*, Ciochon and coauthors John Olsen and Jamie James firmly deny that *Gigantopithecus* ever set foot on North American soil. With the exception of humans, the book says, the last primates to live in North America were squirrel-sized prosimians that became extinct about 25 million years ago.

Other scientists have challenged the claim that Sasquatch and *Gigantopithecus* are basically the same beast. Like its distant cousin the orangutan, *Gigantopithecus* may have been a pseudo-quadruped, or "knuckle-walker," partially carrying itself on four limbs. By contrast, the bulk of the evidence—eyewitness reports, film footage, and footprints—establishes the Sasquatch as a surefooted biped, walking swiftly and efficiently without any help from its arms.

Sasquatch proponents counter that *Gigantopithecus* may not have disappeared during the Pleistocene, as Ciochon rather rigidly maintains. As for the business of quadrupedalism, they claim that *Gigantopithecus* walked upright. According to Krantz, the wide angle of the jawbone indicates that the creature's skull sat atop an erect spinal column.

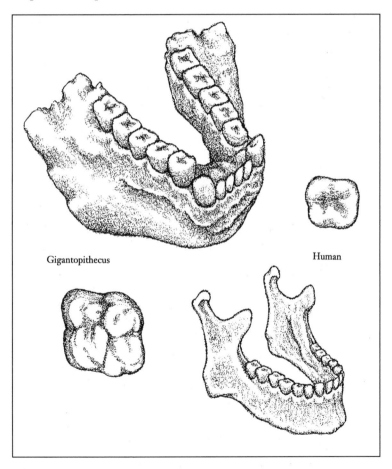

Gigantopithecus   Human

A Sasquatch Profile

DISTRIBUTION Sightings of large, unidentified hominids and their tracks in nearly every North American state and province. Reports are most abundant in British Columbia, Washington, Oregon, northern California, the Great Lakes region, and Florida.

SIZE Height estimates range between 6 and 11 feet (1.8–3.4 m). Weight estimated at 700 to 2,500 pounds (317–1,132 kg).

POSTURE Reported as erect or slightly stooped. No evidence of the quadrupedal locomotion common among other large primates (excluding hominids).

COLORATION Skin color said to be dark. Hair most commonly reported as auburn or black, but also beige, white, and silvery white.

FEATURES Frequently described as monkey- or apelike, with a broad, flattened nose and slitlike, lipless mouth. Sloping forehead is reported to be covered by "bangs" or a fringe of hair; head hair is said to be long, 5 to 7 inches (12.7–17.8 cm). Eyes are thought to reflect light, an adaptation ordinarily associated with nocturnal behavior.

LIMBS Arms are commonly described as elongated, said to swing when walking. Hands have been described as pawlike with thick fingers and hairless palms. Stocky legs, well-muscled, covered with hair.

FOOTPRINT	Said to range from 12 to 22 inches (30.5–55.9 cm) in length, most commonly reported as 14 to 18 inches (35.6–45.7 cm), 7 inches (17.8 cm) in width.
DISPOSITION	Generally reclusive and shy, although alleged to react aggressively when threatened or injured.
FOOD	Presumed omnivorous, able to eat berries, roots, tubers, stems, and other plant material that humans find inedible. Also fond of meat and well-equipped to obtain it; several eyewitnesses tell of Sasquatches carrying deer carcasses, possibly to eat at a later time.
LIFE SPAN	Unknown.

Three Close Encounters
With the Sasquatch

YALE, BRITISH COLUMBIA

"WHAT IS IT?" asked a banner headline of Victoria, British Columbia's *Daily Colonist* on July 4, 1884. "A Strange Creature Captured Above Yale, A British Columbia Gorilla," the paper went on to proclaim.

One of the earliest Sasquatch sightings to be formally documented and, if we are to believe the local press, the only time that humans actually laid hands on a Sasquatch took place near the town of Yale on the Fraser River, the focal point of subsequent Sasquatch reports. According to the *Daily Colonist*, the creature was spied by the crew of a passenger train traveling from the settlement of Lytton to Yale. The train stopped, and the crew, several passengers, and a few Yale townspeople set out in pursuit, corralling the cryptid "after considerable trouble and perilous climbing" on a projecting rock shelf.

Knocked senseless with a piece of rock and bound with the train's bell rope, "Jacko" (as the creature was later called) was loaded into the baggage car and taken to Yale. According to another regional newspaper's account, he was then to be taken to the neighboring town's jail—a rumor that drew a crowd of 200 onlookers. "The only wild man visible was Mr. Moresby, governor of the gaol," quipped the July 12 edition of the New Westminster *Columbian*.

Described by the press as "something of a gorilla type," Jacko stood 4 feet 7 inches (1.4 m) tall and weighed 127 pounds (57.5 kg). His entire body was covered with long, black hair—slightly shorter on his hands and feet—and his forearms were said to be much longer than a man's. During his short stay in Yale, Jacko displayed extraordinary strength, "wrenching and twisting" large sticks and breaking them with ease.

"Who can unravel the mystery that now surrounds Jacko?" wrote the *Daily Colonist*. "Does he belong to a species hitherto unknown in this part of the continent, or is he really what the train men first thought he was, a crazy Indian?" These questions remain unanswered today, as no further mention of Jacko ever appeared in print, nor have any first-person reports been uncovered. One theory has it that Jacko's keepers loaded him into a crate and sent him off to a sideshow in England; the unexplained hominid may have perished en route. Others propose that Jacko was eventually acquired by showman P. T. Barnum, who exhibited a hirsute creature as "Jo-Jo the Dog-Faced Boy" in 1884.

KELSO, WASHINGTON

Human and Sasquatch again came into close contact in the summer of 1924. As reported in the July 13 edition of Portland's *Oregonian*, three prospectors—Marion Smith, his son Roy, and son-in-law Fred Beck—and their companions Gabe Lefevre and John Peterson had seen the tracks and caught glimpses of large, unidentifiable hominids in the wilds of Mount St. Helens in Washington on several occasions over the previous six years. Then, one day, when one of the men fired his rifle at one of these creatures, presumably wounding or killing it, the ill-defined relationship between human and hominid suddenly clarified, taking a decided turn for the worse. That night, the animals reportedly bombarded the prospectors' log cabin with rocks, many of them quite large, knocking chunks out of the cabin and rendering one of the prospectors unconscious.

"The animals were said to have the appearance of huge gorillas," stated *The Oregonian*, echoing the description of Jacko published 40 years earlier. "They are covered with long, black hair. Their ears are about 4 inches long and stick straight up. Their tracks are 13 to 14 inches long. These tracks have been seen by forest rangers and prospectors for years."

According to Beck, the attacks continued throughout the night, with the Sasquatches pounding and trying to get in, and the prospectors shooting their guns through the cabin roof, trying to put an end to the assault. At one point an arm reached in through the cabin's chinking, nearly snatching an ax away from Marion Smith, who fired a round down the ax handle, causing the creature to let go.

Unnerved, the prospectors finally left the cabin for Kelso, filing their report en route. A search party dispatched to the scene of the incident found no signs of Sasquatches or any other giant, apelike beings.

Fred Beck has been interviewed several times in recent years. The interviews suggest that there were at least two creatures outside, and that the attempted shooting of one of them resulted in retaliation.

"Did all this really happen?" asks John Green in *Sasquatch: The Ape Among Us.* "I think so. To the people at that time and place, knowing nothing of such creatures except the old legends of mountain devils at Mount St. Helens, the miners' story was not believable. However, if such creatures do exist, then certainly the most acceptable explanation for the miners having claimed to have seen them is that they did see them. There isn't a shadow of a suggestion as to why they would make up such a story and keep telling it all their lives."

The area around Kelso continues to be a center for Sasquatch sightings and footprint finds. The vicinity of the alleged attacks on the prospectors is now known as Ape Canyon.

BLUFF CREEK, CALIFORNIA

On an autumn day in 1967, two men on horseback rounded the bend of a northern California creek and came face-to-face with a Sasquatch. Roger Patterson and Bob Gimlin were experienced

Sasquatch stalkers; their expedition had been carefully mounted to bring back proof of the cryptid's existence. They had chosen to focus their search on the Bluff Creek drainage, a remote forested site where hundreds of large hominid footprints had supposedly been found, some in creek beds miles from any logging road.

The pair had only been searching for a few days when, in the early afternoon of October 20th, they suddenly encountered the maker of some of these prints—a female Sasquatch, squatting beside the trickling Bluff Creek. Although the creature did not appear to be alarmed at the sight of humans, the two stalkers' horses reacted wildly. Rearing abruptly, Patterson's horse slipped and fell on its side. Patterson raced after his discovery on foot, simultaneously recording its progress with a hand-held 16 mm movie camera. Gimlin stayed put to calm the horses. The excited filmmaker drew within about 80 feet (24.4 m) of the Sasquatch, whose form then became obscured by the trunks of large trees. More footage was taken as the Sasquatch emerged from the trees, but by then it was considerably farther away. Patterson eventually lost sight of his find in the thick forest understory.

The film was received the next day by Patterson's brother-in-law in Yakima, Washington, who took it to Seattle for processing. These 24 feet (7.3 m) of slightly underexposed, somewhat hazy film are now the most celebrated, although highly disputed, evidence of the existence of the Sasquatch ever produced.

The sequence of frames begins with a picture of an animal in profile, striding easefully, arms swinging freely. We see a large-bodied creature of roughly human proportions, covered with dark brown hair. Its head is cone-shaped, perhaps topped with a bony crest (similar to that of adult gorillas, providing supplemental sites of attachment for the large muscles necessitated by massive jaws and teeth). At one point the creature turns to watch

Patterson, performing a full-body swing toward the camera and revealing its bare face and hairy, pendulous breasts. Turning away from the camera, the Sasquatch then strides purposefully away; its prominent buttocks are plainly visible. The sequence ends, to quote physical anthropologist John Napier in his book *Bigfoot: The Yeti and Sasquatch in Myth and Reality*, "for all the world like a classic Charlie Chaplin fade-out," as the Sasquatch walks out of the camera's view and into the vine maples and rhododendrons of Bluff Creek.

Footprints of the Bluff Creek Sasquatch were measured at between 14 and 15 inches (35.6–38 cm), indicating a stature of around 7 feet (2.1 m). The stride was recorded at 41 inches (1.04 m). (By comparison, an adult human stride is under 36 inches.) A wide circle of matted underbrush was also uncovered, indicating that, after the encounter, the cryptid had sat down to watch the two Sasquatch hunters from across the creek, a distance of 125 to 150 yards (114.3–137.2 m).

Although its authenticity is disputed by many members of the scientific community, to date no one has been able to fully discount the Patterson film. Ironically, the biggest uncertainty centers around the speed at which the film was shot. Patterson (who died in 1972) could never confirm whether he had set his camera at 24 feet per second or 16 to 18 feet per second. He was simply too busy to notice. Projected at a slower speed, the motions of a creature filmed at 24 feet per second would appear slow and deliberate. Conversely, at 24 feet per second, the motions of a creature filmed at 16 feet per second would appear quick and erratic. Without an idea of the proper speed for viewing the footage, it is impossible to determine whether the Sasquatch's gait is consistent with that of a human or of an ape. Challengers also cite the unlikely combination of predominantly female (breasts) and male (bony crest) characteristics.

Footprints: Sasquatch Walked Here

Sasquatch footprints have been found just about everywhere: in farmers' fields, outside suburban homes, on mountaintops, and deep in the forests of the United States and Canada. One Sasquatch researcher, John Green of Harrison Hot Springs, British Columbia, has amassed reports of close to 1,000 of what he calls "footprint events"—individual instances in which people and Sasquatches have crossed paths and left footprints to prove it.

At first glance, a Sasquatch footprint looks like a human's in every respect but one—size. The average Sasquatch print is around 7 inches (17.8 cm) wide and 17 or 18 inches (43.2 – 45.7 cm) long. That's more or less the same as a man's size 21 shoe, and even that might pinch a bit, as prints up to 22 inches (55.9 cm) long have been found. That's practically two feet— literally and figuratively.

Even when Sasquatch footprints are the size of our own, it's easy to tell whose feet are whose. Sasquatch prints are quite flat, lacking even the slightest sign of an instep or arch. It's thought that this flatness helps distribute the creature's substantial weight (figured at 700 to 2,500 pounds, 317 – 1,132 kg, for adults) over a large surface area. Sasquatch footprints are usually pressed deep into the ground. Many have twin indents at the base of the big toe, a "double ball" that may be a second load-bearing adaptation of the foot.

In many footprints there's no obvious big toe; rather, equal-size toes are arranged in a fairly straight line. In many others, however, the toes are laid out just like ours, with a bulbous big toe and progressively smaller ones down the line. In his paper "Anatomy of the Sasquatch Foot," published in *Northwest Anthropological Research Notes*, Grover Krantz offers a pair of explanations for the difference in toe types. He proposes first that Sasquatch feet may encompass a great range of variation. Some of the prints also may be fakes, he says, with the impression of the first toe enlarged in order to make them look more convincing.

Which raises a good question: Exactly how many of the footprints now on file have been faked? Without a doubt, many of these crater-sized footprints are man-made, but that doesn't explain away all of them. Several prints show such exceptionally intricate detail, including dermatoglyphic ("fingerprint") patterns, that even a professional fingerprint expert could find no evidence of fakery. In 1983, when Doug Monsoor of the Lakewood, Colorado, police department examined casts of footprints from the Umatilla National Forest, southeast of Walla Walla, Washington, he was impressed with their detailed dermal ridges, the skin patterns that give texture to toe- and fingerprints. Monsoor concluded that "the size, distribution, and orientation of ridge patterns are consistent with those found on the human foot. They appear to be casts of original impressions of a primate foot of a creature that differs from any of which I am aware.... If hoaxing is involved, I can conceive of no way in which it could have been done."

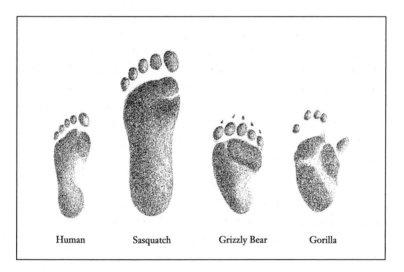

Human   Sasquatch   Grizzly Bear   Gorilla

Another argument for the footprints' validity is the degree to which they reflect the actual dynamics of locomotion, through length of stride, depth of impression, and so forth. To pull off such an effective hoax, a footprint forger would need to be intimately acquainted with the mechanics of walking, particularly among animals of great bulk. Wouldn't anyone with that kind of knowledge be able to put it to better use? Furthermore, many tracks reveal independent toe movement—an attribute that would require extremely sophisticated equipment and an even deeper understanding of biomechanics to fake.

Of special interest is a pair of casts made of footprints found near the town of Bossburg, in northeastern Washington's Colville National Forest. Collected in 1971, the casts reveal a crippling deformity of the right foot—either the middle toe is raised or it is missing altogether, and the entire foot is radically bent inward from the heel. The idea that anyone would think to make anatomically accurate imprints of mangled Sasquatch feet is absurd.

Full and partial handprints have also been found at Sasquatch sites. Roughly twice the size of human hands, these impressions show sturdy, flat fingers and hairless palms. One nearly complete pair of prints found by a Sasquatch tracker in the Blue Mountains of Oregon was impressed in the mud of a streambank, where the animal apparently had steadied itself after falling to one knee. In a second instance, a muddy, 11-inch-long (28 cm) handprint was discovered on the side of a white house in Fort Bragg, California; 16-inch (40.6 cm), four-toed footprints were also discovered in the yard at this site.

Presumed samples of Sasquatch hair and feces have also been collected at several Northwest sites. While some of these were later ascribed to bears or other known forest animals, others cannot be attributed to any known creature. However, attempts to make definitive identifications have been thwarted by the prohibitively high cost of laboratory analysis. Tens of thousands of dollars would have to be spent on gas chromatography/mass spectrometry and other high-tech lab tests before scientifically acceptable data could be obtained. Until these costs are underwritten by the government or a private research foundation, the validity of the samples will remain in question.

Bare Feet or Bear Feet?

It's easy to mistake a bear's footprint for that of a Sasquatch. And because the ranges of both animals overlap, such misidentification is a common occurrence.

Finding the imprint of a large, humanlike sole and five clawless toes is enough to convince many of us that a Sasquatch walked here. But before crying "*Bigfoot!*," look closely at the footprint in question.

A bear's front feet are short, with rounded pads that leave pear-shaped imprints in mud or soft ground. The rear feet are nearly twice as long as the front ones, with narrow heels and insteps that leave imprints that are very human in shape. Both front and rear feet have five thickly padded toes, each of which is tipped with a large, nonretractable claw. But because the claws are raised above the foot pad, a bear can walk without leaving any claw impressions behind, especially if the animal is treading on a very hard surface.

Remember:

- Claw prints are a dead giveaway. No claw marks have ever been found in what are considered genuine Bigfoot footprints.

- A bear's toes are symmetrically placed, unlike a human's, which are asymmetrical and sport a single big toe.

- The vast majority of Sasquatch tracks are longer than 10 inches (25.4 cm), while the rear footprint of a black bear (the most common bear species in the Northwest) seldom exceeds 6 inches (15.2 cm). Even the largest of grizzly bears (a rarely encountered species in Washington, more often encountered in British Columbia) have a rear footprint of less than 14 inches (35.6 cm) —about the same as the smallest Sasquatch tracks.

To Be or Not to Be: Arguments For and Against the Sasquatch

The existence of the Sasquatch has been debated by scientists and Sasquatch watchers for several decades, with heated and occasionally quite personal accusations lodged by both sides. Most members of the scientific community remain unconvinced, citing the lack of evidence to substantiate that such a creature does —or ever did—exist in the Northwest.

The Sasquatch aficionados charge that the scientific community has been lax. They claim that no serious scientific investigations have ever been conducted to confirm or deny their claims; instead, most Sasquatch investigators have been ostracized, branded as kooks for attempting to examine a subject that is largely shunned by standard science.

The scientific establishment bases its case largely on the lack of any Sasquatch skeletons or other remains. The only remnants of the Sasquatch are its footprints, and a certain number of these can be discounted as definite fakes.

That no Sasquatch bones have been found is hardly grounds for dismissal: remains of any large mammal are seldom found in the wild. "Ask any game warden, real woodsman, or professional animal collector if he has ever found the dead body or even a bone of any wild animal—except along roads, of course, or if killed by man," wrote the late naturalist and cryptozoologist Ivan Sanderson in the February 1968 issue of *Argosy* magazine. "I never have, in 40 years on five continents! Nature takes care of its own, and damned fast, too.... " Sanderson and others have argued that the chances of finding the skeleton of a cave-dwelling animal or a creature that ritualistically buried or preserved its dead would be even more slim.

As for the footprints, Sasquatch supporters suggest that, while a number of footprint casts can be discounted as fakes, others have clearly withstood close scrutiny, even by forensics experts. Writing off all of the footprints is unthinkable, comparable to burning all of Rembrandt's paintings because a few forgeries have been uncovered.

Scientists also question the authenticity of eyewitness reports. In these stories, the Sasquatch's reported stature, hair color, means of locomotion, and many other important characteristics vary widely among tellers. Whom are we to believe? And why hasn't the number of Sasquatch sightings increased dramatically with the recreational use and settlement of previously unpopulated wilderness areas?

Again, the Sasquatch side readily concedes that many sightings are invalid, either misidentifications of bears and humans or outright fabrications. But other sightings are not so easily dismissed, having been reported by reputable and knowledgeable individuals. Moreover, the similarities among the reported physical characteristics far outweigh the differences.

Sorting out Sasquatch sightings statistically should be the work of an unbiased third party, but to date no such person or group has stepped forward to tackle this chore. Although public interest in outdoor recreation has boomed over the last 30 years, opportunities for Sasquatch sightings may have been greater in the late 19th century, when prospectors and homesteaders occupied isolated parts of the Northwest for extended periods. Today, the Sasquatch's highly reclusive nature and, possibly, its steadily dwindling population may account for its limited contact with humans in once-remote areas of the Northwest.

Another point of contention is the region's food resources. John Napier has argued that these are inadequate to support a creature the size of a Sasquatch. Despite the density of trees and foliage, writes Napier, the food supply from Northwest forests is generally regarded as meager. Fruits, nuts, and berries are seasonally abundant, but even with a strategy for storing these staples, a creature that depends on these foods is certain to experience some drastically lean seasons. Further south, in northern California, the forest understory is richer, but it still lacks year-round accessible food sources. If the lifestyle and energy needs of the Sasquatch are comparable to those of its presumed relatives, the orangutan and gorilla, then its range would be restricted to tropical climates, where edible plants are available all year long.

Sasquatch scholars are quick to brush this line of thinking aside. They maintain that many large mammals live quite comfortably in Northwest forests. The American elk, for example, survives in winter on a high-fiber diet of twigs, bark, and roots. With its gigantopithecine jawbone and large grinding teeth, the Sasquatch could easily adopt this same strategy during hard times, turning the understory into grist for its rugged dental mill. It has also been suggested that, unlike the tropical gorilla and orangutan (which are both vegetarians), the Sasquatch may be an omnivorous eater, "bulking up" on deer, salmon, rodents, and other high-energy fare. The possibility that the Sasquatch is able to gather and store seasonally abundant foods also should not be dismissed.

Finding a Sasquatch—
And Confirming Your Find

If your single objective is to see a Sasquatch or its tracks, then be prepared for a long, hard haul. With a few notable exceptions (for example, the Patterson-Gimlin expedition of 1967), every organized group effort to observe the creature has failed to provide a glimpse of it. The vast majority of sightings have been chance encounters—startling experiences for both humans and the Sasquatch—most frequently by drivers of vehicles on backcountry roads.

Even for expert trackers there's no guarantee that a week, a month, or a year in the field will produce results. However, amateur Sasquatch stalkers can increase their chances by focusing on locales where sightings have been most numerous and where large, unexplained footprints have been most frequently found. These cryptozoological "hot spots" include the Bluff Creek drainage of northern California, The Dalles in Oregon, the eastern face of Washington's Mount St. Helens, and the Fraser River Valley of southwestern British Columbia.

Statistical analysis of Sasquatch reports has revealed certain peak months for sightings. One study, conducted by Barbara Wasson of Bend, Oregon, pinpointed July for Washington and August for California, Oregon, and British Columbia. Of course, these statistics may only show that greater numbers of people spend their vacations outdoors during summer months; more eyes and ears in the forest would undoubtedly mean more Sasquatch reports. However, from the same analysis a more startling trend has become evident, involving the sequence of summer months in which reported sightings have been lowest—June in California, July in Oregon, August in Washington, and September in British Columbia. This sequence could indicate that as warmer weather starts to spread northward along the West Coast, the

Sasquatch begins to withdraw, perhaps to mate or give birth. Alternatively, the sequence could merely point to some statistical shortcoming resulting from the relatively small sample size (470 separate reports) on which the analysis was based.

If you do happen to spot a Sasquatch or its tracks, the encounter should be accurately and thoroughly documented—only then will your findings be useful to science. First, notify the International Society of Cryptozoology of your sighting. An ISC member can record your detailed observations and, if possible, help find a regional authority on cryptids to assist in any subsequent exploration of the site. (International Society of Cryptozoology, PO Box 43070, Tucson, Arizona, 85733.)

Next, report your find to the local police or sheriff's department. Explain that a discreet investigation of the sighting may be in order. At the same time, *cautiously* contact the local newspaper; a printed story will create a permanent record of the incident. However, it is essential that you inform the newspaper of your desire to avoid creating a media event, which could draw large crowds and obliterate as-yet undiscovered Sasquatch evidence. The local office of the state department of wildlife (or the appropriate arm of state or provincial government) should also be notified. These local natural resource management offices may have already amassed useful information on similar finds in the region.

If a sighting takes place in a remote area, it may be impossible to immediately contact any of the above-mentioned sources. In such instances, every effort should be made to fully document the find. Tape-record or write down a full description of what you saw, including surroundings, time of day, and any other pertinent information. If you are carrying a camera, take plenty of pictures, including a 360-degree sequence of site photos and shots of conspicuous broken branches or other habitat disruptions, as well as any signs of food gathering or consumption.

If you find footprints, be sure to photograph a sequence of steps in addition to close-ups of both the left and right feet. For close-ups your camera should be positioned directly above the print, to reduce distortion. Place some readily recognizable object (a pocket knife, for example) near each footprint to establish its scale. If possible, record the length and width of each print, the distance between prints, and the total area over which the prints are spread. It is important to photograph more than one print made by the same foot; by interpreting these multiple images, investigators may be able to infer much about an individual animal's build and behavior. Photographs that show the footprints in their larger setting can also aid in this interpretation.

If plaster or other casting materials are available, impressions should be taken of the most intact footprints or handprints. Impressions of partial prints should also be taken if casting materials are ample. If it is impossible to make casts, the positions of the footprints should be marked and the prints protected from wind, rain, and trampling by humans or animals.

Guide to Listings

No single, comprehensive directory of Sasquatch sightings currently exists. In the past, data has been compiled by a number of individuals and organizations throughout North America, who may or may not freely share their records.

The listings in this book have come from several sources, primarily the comprehensive files of Canadian Sasquatch scholar John Green. As of this writing, Green's files contain reports of more than 800 Sasquatch sightings and 2,500 footprint incidents in the greater Northwest.

For the purpose of substantiation, only reports that have been documented by newspapers and other published sources have been included in the listings. Efforts have been taken to present those reports that have withstood initial investigation and that illustrate some facet of Sasquatch behavior—either directly observed or inferred.

Listings are arranged geographically, by state and province, and chronologically, from the distant past to the present day. Each listing is numbered for easy location on the accompanying map.

Should you encounter a Sasquatch or discover humanlike footprints of unusual size or shape, we'd like to hear from you. All reports will be treated confidentially. Send information about your find to:

Sasquatch Books
1931 Second Avenue
Seattle, WA 98101

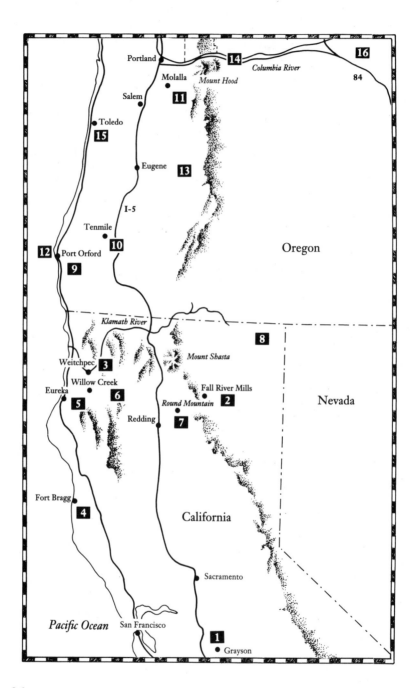

Northern California

November 1870

A detailed account of a sighting of a hairy, 5-foot-tall (1.5 m), reddish brown "gorilla or wildman" appears in *The Butte Record*. According to the report, the creature whistled, played with burning sticks from a hunter's fire, and was later joined by a similar female. **1**

May 1947

A married couple reports seeing, on a fishing trip south of Fall River Mills, two dark, hair-covered creatures walking along the bank, gathering and eating fish and reeds in a canyon. Tracks left in the mud measure 17½ inches (44.5 cm) and 14 inches (35.6 cm) long. **2**

August 1958

Twenty miles (32 km) north of the Klamath River, between Orleans and Weitchpec, a road crew repeatedly finds trails of 16-inch-long (40.6 cm) footprints. A brief story and a photograph of a plaster cast of one of the prints is carried by the *Humboldt Times*, which coins the term "Bigfoot" to describe the creature that supposedly made the prints. When the story is picked up by the Associated Press, this name gains widespread recognition. **3**

June 1962

Following a nocturnal Sasquatch sighting, a muddy handprint 11½ inches (29.2 cm) across is discovered on the side of a Fort Bragg home. **4**

August 1967

On two occasions, a crew finds 13- and 15-inch (33 and 36 cm) tracks at work sites near Onion Mountain and Blue Creek Mountain. The makers of the prints seem to have been curious about human activity: at one site, footprints are photographed near a water wagon; at the other, small tractor parts are found scattered along the road. **5**

OCTOBER 1967

Sasquatch stalkers Roger Patterson and Bob Gimlin return from their horseback expedition to Bluff Creek with film footage of an alleged adult female Sasquatch. Subsequent investigation of the discovery site reveals 14½-inch (36.8 cm) footprints spread out over several hundred yards of terrain. In the vicinity of Bluff Creek, numerous Sasquatch reports are filed over the following two years. One party of hikers reports seeing more than a thousand 16-inch (40.6 cm) tracks in the snow, near where bark had been stripped from trees. **6**

JANUARY 1971

Four-toed humanoid footprints are found in the yard of a home on Round Mountain in Shasta County. The prints are reported as 18 inches (45.7 cm) long and 7 inches (17.8 cm) wide. The following December, three Forest Service workers discover 30-inch-long (76.2 cm), 10-inch-wide (25.4 cm) tracks in deep snow on a road to Camp Creek, near the town of Orleans. The stride measures 5 feet (1.5 m), according to the *Klamity Kourier.* **7**

JUNE 1989

The *Sacramento Bee* reports an encounter between an 8-foot-tall (2.4 m) Bigfoot and a resident of the Fort Bidwell Indian Reservation in Modoc County. The resident was keeping watch outside a relative's home, where one or more Bigfoots had allegedly been seen on previous nights. According to the *Bee*, the creature charged the resident, who was able to repel the attack by shining his flashlight in the Bigfoot's highly reflective eyes. No further sightings were reported. **8**

Oregon

MARCH 1904

Three sightings of the "Wild Man" of the Sixes are reported in one month, according to the *Lane County Leader.* The Sixes' Sasquatch is said to be 7 feet (2.1 m) tall and covered with a thick growth of hair. The newspaper article also describes several aggressive acts, including rock throwing and the shaking of a cabin, by the creature. **9**

OCTOBER 1959

Two boys tell of firing their guns at a Sasquatch, which appears to have been trying to drive them away from a wilderness site south of Tenmile. The gunshots do little to deter the creature, which, according to the boys, "screamed like a cat, but louder," continuing to follow them. Eventually the alleged Sasquatch gives up the chase. Casts are later made of strangely shaped, five-toed footprints 11½ inches (29.2 cm) long and 8 inches (20.3 cm) wide at the toes. **10**

OCTOBER 1967

In the Cascade mountains, southeast of Molalla, a logger claims to have encountered two adults and one juvenile Sasquatch digging holes near a rock pile. Awestruck, he watches as the trio captures and devours several of what are presumed to be hibernating ground squirrels. The next year, the same logger witnesses a Sasquatch stripping leaves from a willow bush and eating them. Subsequent investigations of this region and of similar montane habitats in Oregon reveal dozens of holes, possibly dug by rooting Sasquatches. **11**

AUGUST 1969

The Sixes Wild Man lives, according to a scuba diver. The diver reports that, as he was busily dredging a stream near Port Orford, the creature sat for about 30 minutes with its huge head in its hand and an elbow on its knee, watching the dredging operation. **12**

JUNE 1972

East of Eugene, tree fellers report seeing a hairy, dark brown creature, estimated to be 7 feet (2.1 m) tall, standing among the trees they cut the day before. Upon discovery, the supposed Sasquatch quickly walks into the forest and out of sight. The next month, a surveyor discovers a similar creature squatting in a clearing and staring at the surveyor's dog. Again, the Sasquatch retreats rapidly when confronted by a human. **13**

JULY 1974

Members of a logging crew on Fir Mountain in the Hood River County Forest see a Sasquatch on two consecutive days. Pursuing his burly 6- to 6½-foot (1.8 – 2 m) find on foot, one of the crew members throws rocks at the fast-moving creature. Undeterred by the barrage, the Sasquatch escapes into dense scrub. **14**

SEPTEMBER 1979

The *Oregon Journal* prints the story of five hunters who claim to have seen a large hominid with orange-brown hair lurking around their campsite in the Burnt Woods near Toledo. According to the *Journal*, large handprints were later found on the hunters' trucks. **15**

JUNE 1982

A U.S. Forest Service patrolman claims he encountered, while on a routine patrol of the Mill Creek Watershed in the Umatilla National Forest, an 8-foot-tall (2.4 m), 800-pound (362.4 kg) Sasquatch bounding down a logging spur road. Casts made of the creature's footprints are highly detailed, with convincingly authentic dermal ridges that withstand the scrutiny of forensics experts. **16**

Washington

JULY 1924

Four prospectors claim to have survived an attack on their cabin near Kelso by apelike creatures. According to the Portland *Oregonian*, the attackers "were said to have the appearance of huge gorillas.... Their tracks are 13 to 14 inches long." The site of the alleged skirmish is subsequently named Ape Canyon. **17**

SUMMER 1955 OR 1956

Ten people on a hike from a YMCA camp at Spirit Lake report seeing a large, upright creature—taller than a man and with longish, dirty white hair—at the edge of a meadow between Coldwater Lookout and St. Helens Lake. Startled, the creature runs away, "leaping like an Olympic hurdles champ over fallen logs," in the words of one eyewitness. **18**

JULY 1963

The *Oregon Journal* runs a story about its business editor, who claims to have seen a Sasquatch while driving his car through Satus Pass. The editor's claim is confirmed by two passengers, who report having seen the creature step up from a roadside ditch once the car passed. The next month, the *Journal* prints a report about a group of Boy Scouts being badly frightened but unharmed by an "ape man" on Mount St. Helens in the early 1940s. **19**

SEPTEMBER–DECEMBER 1967

Ten separate Sasquatch sightings are logged by local fishermen and residents of the Nooksack River delta near Marietta. In all but three, the creature is spotted entering, swimming in, or leaving the river—possibly to partake of the sockeye salmon run. One of these reports describes the Sasquatch reeling in a fisherman's gillnet. **20**

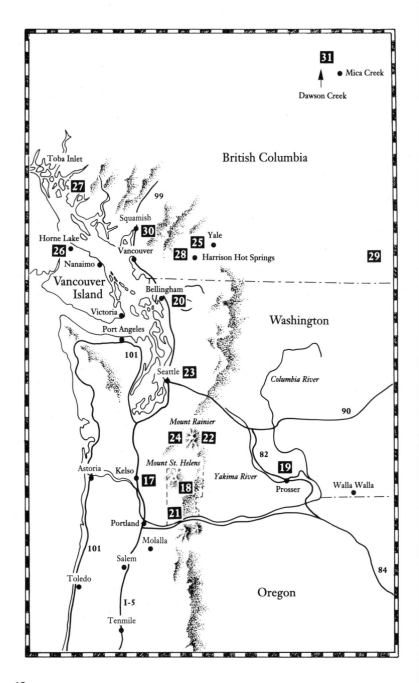

31

• Mica Creek

↑

Dawson Creek

British Columbia

Toba Inlet

27

99

Squamish

30

Horne Lake

26

Nanaimo

Vancouver

Yale

25

28

• Harrison Hot Springs

29

Vancouver
Island

Bellingham

20

Victoria

Washington

Port Angeles

101

Columbia River

Seattle 23

90

Mount Rainier

24 22

Mount St. Helens

82

19

Astoria

Kelso

Yakima River

17

Prosser

Walla Walla

18

Portland

21

Molalla

84

Salem

Toledo

Oregon

I-5

Tenmile

42

APRIL 1969

Following an outbreak of Sasquatch sightings and footprint dis-
coveries, the Board of County Commissioners of Skamania
County passes the world's first Sasquatch Protection Ordinance.
This ordinance states that "there is evidence to indicate the
possible existence in Skamania County of a nocturnal primate
mammal variously described as an ape-like creature or a sub-
species of Homo Sapiens, and...both legend and purported
recent sightings and spoor support this possibility." It provides
that "any premeditated, wilful and wanton slaying of any such
creature shall be deemed a felony punishable by a fine not to exceed Ten Thousand Dollars ($10,000.00) and/or imprisonment
in the county jail for a period not to exceed Five (5) years." To
date, no violators of the ordinance have been prosecuted. **21**

JULY 1970

On a trail between Sunrise Point and Mystic Lake, two hikers
in Mount Rainier National Park reportedly cross paths with an
8-foot-tall (2.4 m), bipedal mammal covered with brown hair.
The face of the creature is described as apelike, its walk slightly
bent at the waist and knees. **22**

FEBRUARY 1985

Two sets of tracks are discovered in a subdivision in Bellevue,
apparently left by large, barefooted beings. The tracks indicate
that as the creatures walked, they stopped to peer into the win-
dows of several homes on both sides of the street. Individual
footprints are reported to be 24½ inches (62.2 cm) and 18
inches (45.7 cm) long. **23**

SEPTEMBER 1990

Mushroom hunters on a slope of Mount Rainier above National
report finding a line of 15-inch (38 cm) footprints in a creek bed.
24

British Columbia

JULY 1884

"Jacko," a 4-foot-7-inch (1.4 m) ape-man, is captured by a train crew north of Yale and placed in the town jail. No record of Jacko's subsequent fate has been found. **25**

DECEMBER 1904

The *Victoria Daily Colonist* describes the discovery by area residents of a wild man in the vicinity of Horne Lake on Vancouver Island: "The wild man was apparently young, with long matted hair and a beard, and covered with a profusion of hair all over his body. He ran like a deer through the seemingly impenetrable tangle of undergrowth, and pursuit was utterly impossible." **26**

SUMMER 1924

A hunter near Toba Inlet maintains he was nabbed in his sleeping bag, carried off, and held captive by a Sasquatch family for several days. Thirty years later, the hunter signs a statutory declaration supporting his oft-quoted account of Sasquatch home life. **27**

OCTOBER 1941

Convinced that a Sasquatch is chasing them, a mother and two young children flee from their home in the remote Ruby Creek area. Sixteen-inch (40.6 cm) footprints are later found circling the house and entering a shed nearby. For the next 50 years, the Ruby Creek area continues to be a hotbed of Sasquatch sightings. **28**

OCTOBER 1960

The *Nelson Daily News* describes an encounter between two berry pickers—Sasquatch and human—north of Nelson. The "great beast" is said to be covered with bluish gray hair, with its height estimated at 7 to 9 feet (2.1–2.7 m). **29**

APRIL 1969

Workers on a ski development north of Squamish uncover several miles of 14-inch (35.6 cm) footprints in the snow. It is suggested that the tracks' maker was stripping spruce buds off the trees and eating them. Eight months later, an automobile driver reports seeing a 7-foot (2.1 m) hairy hominid in the same vicinity. The creature is said to have been running across the road, carrying a small fish in its hands. **30**

MARCH 1987

On several occasions, four members of a gas drilling operation southwest of Dawson Creek witness a Sasquatch-like being moving through the trees. The creature is said to leave many large footprints behind. **31**

To Learn More About the Sasquatch

BOOKS:

Janet and Colin Bord, *Bigfoot Casebook* (Harrisburg, PA: Stackpole Books, 1982)

Russell Ciochon, John Olsen, and Jamie James, *Other Origins: The Search for the Giant Ape in Human Prehistory* (New York: Bantam Books, 1990)

John Green, *Sasquatch: The Apes Among Us* (Saanichton, B.C., and Seattle: Hancock House Publishers Ltd., 1978)

John Napier, *Bigfoot: The Yeti and Sasquatch in Myth and Reality* (New York: E. P. Dutton & Co. Inc., 1972)

Ivan T. Sanderson, *Abominable Snowmen: Legend Come to Life* (Philadelphia: Chilton Company, 1961)

JOURNAL:

International Society of Cryptozoology, *Cryptozoology: The Interdisciplinary Journal of the International Society of Cryptozoology* (Tucson: annual, by subscription)